LET'S FIND OUT! SPORTS

WHAT IS SOCCER?

I0807761

JOE GASPAR

Britannica Educational Publishing
IN ASSOCIATION WITH
ROSEN
EDUCATIONAL SERVICES

Published in 2019 by Britannica Educational Publishing (a trademark of Encyclopædia Britannica, Inc.) in association with The Rosen Publishing Group, Inc.
29 East 21st Street, New York, NY 10010

Copyright © 2019 The Rosen Publishing Group, Inc. and Encyclopædia Britannica, Inc. Encyclopædia Britannica, Britannica, and the Thistle logo are registered trademarks of Encyclopædia Britannica, Inc. All rights reserved.

Distributed exclusively by Rosen Publishing.
To see additional Britannica Educational Publishing titles, go to rosenpublishing.com.

First Edition

Britannica Educational Publishing
J.E. Luebering: Executive Director, Core Editorial
Mary Rose McCudden: Editor, Britannica Student Encyclopedia

Rosen Publishing
Amelie von Zumbusch: Editor
Brian Garvey: Series Designer/Book Layout
Cindy Reiman: Photography Manager

Library of Congress Cataloging-in-Publication Data

Names: Gaspar, Joe, author.
Title: What is soccer? / Joe Gaspar.
Description: First Edition. | New York : Britannica Educational Publishing, in association with Rosen Educational Services, 2019. | Series: Let's find out! Sports | Includes bibliographical references and index.
Identifiers: LCCN 2018029379 | ISBN 9781538304761 (library bound)
ISBN 9781538304808 (pbk.) | ISBN 9781538304891 (6 pack)
Subjects: LCSH: Soccer—Juvenile literature.
Classification: LCC GV943.25 .G35 2019 | DDC 796.334—dc23
LC record available at https://lccn.loc.gov/2018029379

Manufactured in the United States of America

Photo credits: Cover, interior pages background Eugene Onischenk/Shutterstock.com; p. 4 Africa Studio/Shutterstock.com; p. 5 Jefferson Bernardes/Shutterstock.com; p. 6 © Merriam-Webster Inc.; p. 7 CLS Digital Arts/Shutterstock.com; p. 8 imagestockdesign/Shutterstock.com; p. 9 ShutterOK/Shutterstock.com; p. 10 Shawn Pecor/Shutterstock.com; p. 11 Oleksandr Osipov/Shutterstock.com; p. 12 Review News/Shutterstock.com; p. 13 Albo/Shutterstock.com; p. 14 barbsimages/Shutterstock.com; p. 15 Monkey Business Images/Shutterstock.com; p. 16 Popperfoto/Getty Images; p. 17 Stuart Franklin-FIFA/Getty Images; p. 18 Csaba Peterdi/Shutterstock.com; pp. 19, 29 Ververidis Vasilis/Shutterstock.com; p. 20 Laurence Griffiths/Getty Images; p. 21 Fethi Belaid/AFP/Getty Images; p. 22 David Cannon/David Cannon Collection/Getty Images; p. 23 Maddie Meyer-FIFA/Getty Images; p. 24 lev radin/Shutterstock.com; p. 25 Photo Works/Shutterstock.com; p. 26 A. Ricardo/Shutterstock.com; p. 27 Paul Popper/Popperfoto/Getty Images; p. 28 Ezra Shaw/Getty Images.

Contents

Let's Play Soccer!

Soccer is the world's most popular team sport. In most parts of the world the game is called football or association football. Both men and women play soccer in schools, clubs, and on national and professional teams. In a soccer game, two teams compete to score more points, which are called goals. The players move the ball around a rectangular field, usually by kicking it. A team scores when it sends the ball

Many people are drawn to the athletic skill and quick thinking that soccer requires.

into the opposing team's goal.

Games like soccer were played in China more than two thousand years ago. Similar games were played in ancient Greece, Rome, Japan, and Mexico. But the modern game of soccer started in England in the nineteenth century.

The World Cup soccer tournament is the world's most popular sports event. Every four years teams from many countries compete for the World Cup.

Billions of people around the world watch teams from different countries compete in the World Cup.

Compare and Contrast

How are team sports like individual sports? In what ways are they different?

Field and Equipment

Soccer fields vary in size. A field should be 100 to 130 yards (90 to 120 meters) long and 50 to 100 yards (45 to 90 m) wide. Boundary lines called touchlines mark the sides of the field. Goal lines mark the ends of the field. A goal is located at each end of the field. The goal is a

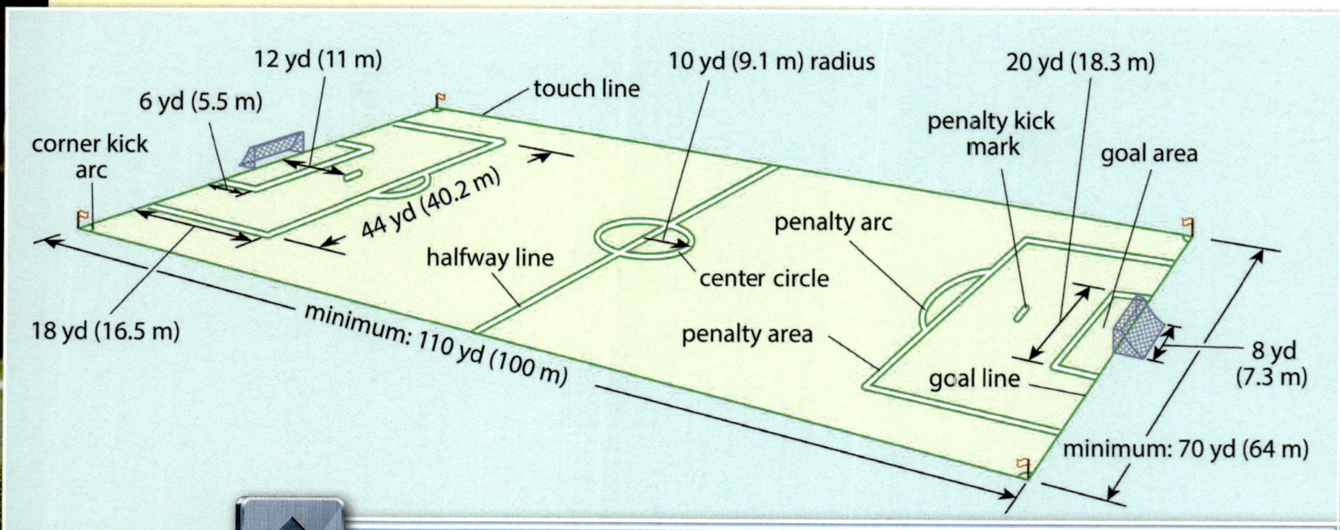

For international soccer matches the field should be 110 to 130 yards long and 70 to 80 yards wide.

frame that is 8 yards (7.3 m) wide and 8 feet (2.4 m) high. It has a net on the top, sides, and back. A soccer ball is round and filled with air.

Soccer teams have eleven players. Each team tries to control the ball and move it toward the opponent's goal. Only one player on each team, the goalkeeper, can touch the ball with the hands and arms. The other players can touch the ball with any other body part. They usually move the ball with their feet.

Soccer uniforms are most often shorts, a shirt with a number, socks, shoes with cleats, and shin guards.

Think About It

Why do you think goalkeepers are allowed to touch the ball with their hands?

Player Positions

During a soccer game, the players of each team spread across the field in loose formations. A formation generally has front, back, and middle sections.

The front section is the offensive, or scoring, part of the team. The main offensive players are called forwards, or strikers. When a team has the ball, the forwards try to score goals. A team's forwards are usually located closest to the opponent's goal.

Cristiano Ronaldo is one of the world's most famous professional soccer forwards.

Goalkeepers are often called goalies. Their job is to stop the opponent's ball from getting into the net.

The back section is mostly defensive—it protects the team's goal. Each team has a goalkeeper in front of its goal. Goalkeepers try to deflect or catch the opponent's shots at the goal. Players called defenders form a defensive screen between their goalkeeper and the opposing team. Defenders try to take the ball from the other team.

The players in the middle section play both offense and defense. Midfielders generally are located between their team's forwards and defenders.

Compare and Contrast

How are the roles of forwards and defenders different? What do they have in common?

Soccer Skills

Soccer players move the ball by dribbling, kicking, or heading it. A player dribbles by using very short kicks to move the ball forward. Dribbling allows a player to keep control of the ball while running down the field. Players use longer kicks to pass the ball to teammates or to try to make a goal. Striking the ball with the head is called heading.

Heading is one way to move the ball down the field. However, it is not safe for pre-teen players.

Players have several ways to take control of the ball from the other team.

Players often head the ball when receiving long, high passes. Sometimes they also try to head the ball into the goal.

When one player has the ball, players on the opposing team try to take the ball away from that player. This is called tackling. In one type of tackle a player uses the feet to kick or steal the ball away from an opponent. Another way to get the ball is by intercepting a pass.

Vocabulary

Intercepting a pass is getting to the ball before the opponent can get to it.

Fouls and Penalties

Three officials—a referee and two assistants—control the game. They give teams **penalties** when players commit fouls, or break the rules. After some fouls the officials award free kicks to the other team. When a free kick is taken, all players of the offending team must be at least 10 yards (9 meters)

Vocabulary

Penalties are punishments for doing something wrong.

Referees can show cards when players commit fouls. Red cards get players ejected from a game.

from the ball. The officials award penalty kicks for more serious fouls. A penalty kick is a free kick at the offending team's goal. It is taken from a spot 12 yards (11 meters) from the goal. All players other than the defending goalkeeper and the kicker must stand aside.

It is easier to score on a penalty kick because only the goalkeeper can defend against it.

One common foul is being offside. An offensive player cannot pass the two defenders closest to the goal until the ball is played to him. The rule keeps players from lurking around the goal all game. When offside is called, a free kick is awarded to the defensive team.

Youth Soccer

Many children and teens around the world enjoy playing soccer. It is a common activity in gym classes. Many schools also have soccer teams that compete against teams from other schools.

Kids can also join their local soccer association or club. The two biggest youth soccer organizations in the United States are US Youth Soccer and the American Youth Soccer Organization (AYSO). In Canada, kids

Soccer is a popular sport for children around the world.

and teens can progress through the early levels of the Canada Soccer Pathway.

Youth soccer players both practice with their teams and play games against other teams. Players under the age of twelve or thirteen may play small-sided games. These are games in which each side has fewer than eleven players. The younger the players are, the fewer kids there tend to be in each side. Young players also use smaller fields and smaller balls.

High schools may have several soccer teams, at different levels of competitiveness.

Think About It

Why might soccer teams with young players have fewer players?

SOCCER HISTORY

This image from about 1881 shows some of the stars from the early years of FA competition.

In 1863 several English soccer teams formed the Football Association (FA). It created the first standard set of rules for the game.

The FA was an amateur organization, which means that its players were not paid. Professional soccer leagues, in which players were paid, began in the late 1880s. They formed first in England and then in other countries. By 1900 people were playing soccer throughout the world.

In 1904 the Fédération Internationale de Football Association (FIFA) was formed. FIFA governs the game at the international level. In 1930 FIFA organized the first World Cup tournament. The first women's World Cup was held in 1991.

Soccer became an official event at the Olympic Games in 1908. It was the first team sport to be included in the Olympics. Women's soccer became an Olympic event in 1996.

COMPARE AND CONTRAST

How is the World Cup like the Olympics? In what ways is it different?

Brazil beat Germany to win the gold medal in men's soccer at the Olympic Games in 2016.

Soccer Around the World

Fans around the world pack stadiums to watch their favorite soccer teams play.

Soccer is a wildly popular sport. It has been estimated that at the turn of the twenty-first century there were some 240 million soccer players around the globe and more than 1.3 billion fans.

Soccer has been played in almost every Summer Olympics since 1908. The true world championship, however, is the FIFA-run World Cup. It is played every four years and is the most-watched sporting event in the world.

FIFA has more than 200 member nations worldwide. It is divided into six continental confederations (Africa, Asia, Europe, North America, South America, and Oceania). These oversee national team competition and club play in their own regions. These confederations present their own international cup tournaments, such as the European Cup and the African Nations Cup. They also oversee major club competitions, including the Champions League tournament in Europe and South America's Copa America.

Real Madrid won the Union of European Football Associations' UEFA Super Cup in 2017.

Think About It

Why do you think there are so many different soccer tournaments?

The World Cup

Germany has won the FIFA World Cup several times, including in 2014.

The World Cup is a championship tournament for soccer teams around the world. Different countries take turns hosting the event, which is held every four years. It draws billions of television viewers every tournament.

The tournament lasts for several weeks. The competition to qualify as a World Cup team lasts for much longer. Many teams

VOCABULARY

A **trophy** is something given in recognition of a victory.

The qualifying matches for the 2018 World Cup started in 2015.

compete in qualifying tournaments by region over the course of about two years. Eventually thirty-two teams qualify to compete for the men's trophy. There are twenty-four teams in the women's tournament.

The teams are placed in groups of four teams each. In the first round, each team plays the other three in its group. The top two teams from each group advance to the next round. In the next three rounds teams are eliminated as they play each other. Referees for the

World Cup tournament are selected from lists that are submitted by all the national associations.

Uruguay won the first men's World Cup in 1930. The event has been held every four years since then, except during World War II. The trophy cup awarded from 1930 to 1970 was the Jules Rimet Trophy. It was named for the Frenchman who proposed the tournament. This cup was permanently awarded in 1970 to then three-time winner

THINK ABOUT IT

Can you guess why the World Cup was not held during World War II?

Brazil got to keep the Jules Rimet Trophy after it was awarded in 1970.

Brazil (1958, 1962, and 1970). A new trophy called the FIFA World Cup was then put up for competition. In 2018 Russia was the host country for the event. France was the winning team.

In 2015, the US women's soccer team won the FIFA Women's World Cup for the third time.

In 1991 FIFA held the first women's World Cup tournament. Like the men's tournament, it has been held every four years since then. The US women's team has won the tournament several times. France was selected to host the 2019 tournament.

Soccer in North America

Many people in the United States enjoy playing soccer. Nevertheless watching professional soccer is not as popular in North America as it is in other parts of the world. In the 1990s, however, it began to grow in popularity.

In 1994 the United States hosted the World Cup. Two years later a professional

The MLS teams in this 2017 match were the New York Red Bulls and the Montreal Impact.

league—Major League Soccer (MLS)—was formed. The league includes Canadian teams as well as US ones. Its teams are split up into two divisions, known as the Eastern Conference and the Western Conference. The league even attracted international football stars—including David Beckham, Thierry Henry, and Hristo Stoichkov—to play in it.

Think About It

Why do you think soccer isn't more popular in the United States? What sports do Americans watch instead?

DC United won the league's first championship game (known as the MLS Cup) in 1996. That club and the Los Angeles Galaxy have captured the most league titles.

English star David Beckham played for the Los Angeles Galaxy between 2007 and 2012.

Amazing Players

If they had to pick the greatest player of all, many soccer fans would agree on Pelé. This Brazilian player's career stretched from 1956 to 1977. He is known for his tremendous speed and balance, his jumping and ball-controlling abilities, and his spectacular goals. During his career Pelé played in 1,363 games and scored 1,281 goals.

The Dutch forward Johan Cruyff is known for his imaginative

Pelé was born in Três Corações, Brazil. His real name is Edson Arantes do Nascimento.

play making. He won many awards, including European Footballer of the Year in 1971, 1973, and 1974.

One of the most famous players of the 1980s, Diego Maradona became a hero to the poor in his native Argentina. He led teams from Argentina, Spain, and Italy to championship wins, including Argentina's 1986 World Cup success. He played 490 official club games during his 21-year professional career, scoring 259 goals.

A loyal Argentine, Maradona played on his homeland's World Cup teams in 1982, 1986, 1990, and 1994.

Think About It

What skills and qualities do you think make a soccer player truly great?

Mia Hamm *(left)* helped the US team win a gold medal in women's soccer in the 2004 Olympics.

FIFA named Mia Hamm the Women's World Player of the Year in both 2001 and 2002. A powerful striker, she held the record for the most international goals (158) of any player—male or female—in the history of the sport until 2013. Aside from her knack for goal-scoring, Hamm is revered for her all-around skill and competitive spirit.

Portuguese soccer player Cristiano Ronaldo is considered one of the best soccer players of his generation. He signed with an English team, Manchester United, in 2003. His finest season with the team came in 2007–08, when he earned the Golden Shoe award as Europe's leading scorer. Ronaldo also played for the Portuguese national team.

The Argentine-born Lionel Messi was named FIFA world player of the year multiple times, including four years in a row from 2009 to 2012. Though only 5 feet 7 inches (1.7 meters) tall, he is strong, well-balanced, and versatile on the field.

VOCABULARY

A versatile player is skilled at many things.

Lionel Messi is known for his keen passing and precise ball control.

Glossary

assistant A person who helps another.

club A group of people who get together because of a common interest; professional soccer teams are known as clubs.

defense The part of a team that tries to keep the other team from scoring.

formation The pattern in which things or people are arranged.

foul Breaking a rule in a game or sport.

goal An area or object into which a ball or puck must be driven to score points in various games.

goalkeeper The player who defends the goal.

knack A skill or talent.

offense The part of a team that tries to score.

play making Coming up with offensive moves in a sport.

precise Very exact.

professional Taking part for money in an activity (as sport) that others do for pleasure.

propose To suggest or recommend.

qualify To earn a spot in a competition.

referee A sports official usually having final authority in conducting a game.

revere To honor and think highly of.

submit To present to another for review or decision.

tackle To grab something, especially to stop or slow it down.

tournament A contest or series of contests played for a championship.

For More Information

Books

Bader, Bonnie. *What Is the World Cup?* New York, NY: Penguin Workshop, 2018.

Hammelef, Danielle S. *First Source to Soccer: Rules, Equipment, and Key Playing Tips.* North Mankato, MN: Capstone Press, 2018.

Mikoley, Kate. *Soccer: Stats, Facts, and Figures.* New York, NY: Gareth Stevens Publishing, 2018.

Nagelhout, Ryan. *Soccer: Who Does What?* New York, NY: Gareth Stevens Publishing, 2018.

Savage, Jeff. *US Women's National Team: Soccer Champions* (Champion Soccer Clubs). Minneapolis, MN: Lerner Publications, 2019.

Websites

American Youth Soccer Organization
http://www.ayso.org/
Facebook: @AYSOsoccer;
Twitter: @AYSO_Soccer

Canada Soccer
https://www.canadasoccer.com/
Facebook: @canadasoccer;
Twitter: @CanadaSoccerEN

FIFA
http://grassroots.fifa.com/en/for-kids.html
Facebook: @fifa; Twitter: @FIFAcom

US Youth Soccer
https://www.usyouthsoccer.org/
Facebook and Twitter: @USYouthSoccer

INDEX